THE SILENT STARS GO BY

THE SILENT STARS GO BY

A True Christmas Story

Philip Lee Williams

d

HILL STREET PRESS   ATHENS, GEORGIA

HILL STREET PRESS
Published by Hill Street Press, LLC
191 East Broad Street
Suite 209
Athens, Georgia 30601-2848
www.hillstreetpress.com

First printing

1 3 5 7 9 10 8 6 4 2

ISBN # 1-892514-07-9

Printed in the United States of America by R. R. Donnelley & Sons
Company.

Set in 11/13 Centaur.

The paper in this book contains a significant amount of post-consumer
recycled fiber.

Text and cover design by Anne Richmond Boston.

For my parents, Ruth and Woody Williams,
and for Laura Jane and Mark

foreword

It is beyond human ability to remember day-to-day details of one holiday that occurred nearly forty years ago. Much of that time remains strong in my memory, however, because my life changed not long afterward. Still, this book is presented as a series of images rather than a strict narrative because it is the most honest way I can approach that very memorable Christmas of 1959.

one

*

First were the fields and the night sky. The green of pine and cedar filled us, and brown furrows folded back with spring's enduring promise protected us. Autumn in north Georgia was a treasure of drifting wind, the sharp smell of burning leaves. Lucky children often retreat to the beauty and solitude of childhood images, and I was among the luckiest in north Georgia the late fall and early winter of 1959, as much for what I did not know as for what I did.

The leaves had released their summer hold on the tree limbs. They lay in bronze and yellow piles or simply drifted with the wind currents. We burned great mounds of brown water oak leaves in our yard, and I imagine my mother, still as a painting, leaning on her rake and watching flames turn those flakes of leaf into an aroma rich enough to taste.

This is what I knew: A close and loving family, a mother and father I loved and admired, a brother who was my friend, and a new sister, born the end of September and starting to be all smiles. Yet in a sense, I sometimes felt a stretch of loneliness, the pale whisper of years passing. I thought of my father's parents, both of whom had died before I was born in

1950, and I thought of South Carolina, where my closest relatives lived, one hundred miles distant. But mostly I lived in the sincerity of my parents' love, the certainties of faith, and the comfort of country.

I had been shaken by the death of a favorite uncle a year before, but the life we lived at the country's welcoming edge, just outside Madison in the Georgia Piedmont, would continue always, I assumed. My father was principal of Morgan County High School, and I entered his office with awe and respect, knowing he was a famous man. I was a dreamy child, given to reading and music, filled with a potent desire to flee into the woods, to get away from man-made sounds. I found the silence of the forest intoxicating. In high summer, when the hawks hunted low in the pasture behind our house for field mice, I would set out with a canteen and a peanut butter sandwich and spend an entire day exploring in the pine woods owned by the county. I did not mind being alone, though my brother or friends sometimes went, too. The best days I spent exploring, looking for signs.

That fall of 1959 uncurled with leaf-smoke like any other. There were school and church and family. I had begun to touch the ivory keys of our piano with a yearning to make music, but I could not yet play as my father did. My life was more consumed with another passion: football. We had little money in those times, and my father, even as a high school principal, barely made enough to support a family of five. I only knew I wanted a red football uniform for Christmas.

I was unsure I would get it, but I tried to be good and waited for the seasonal ritual of an early December walk to the woods to find and cut a Christmas tree. I knew nothing of liturgical symbolism; I only knew that the aroma of cedar was entangled in my southern heart with love, religion, anxiety, and a deep sense of closeness and peace.

My parents, Ruth and Woody, were thirty-five and thirty-seven respectively that December, and my brother Mark had turned eleven in August. I was nine, in love with the fields and the woods, venturing farther each day on my bicycle along the dirt roads of Morgan County, some sixty miles east of Atlanta. I liked school, thrived in the fourth grade, and often I sat on the back porch of our house and watched the moon as it slowly swung up on a cricket chorus and settled into a nesting bed of stars.

I could not wait until we sought that perfect cedar. I did not guess this would be the last Christmas tree I would ever help cut in that precious country of childhood.

two

W_e moved to that frame house in August of 1953 when Daddy became a chemistry and physics teacher at Morgan County High School. I was three years old then and so remember little from those years but occasional scenes, frozen like Matthew Brady photographs. I have often wondered why we cannot remember our earliest years. I can only say that I awoke to boyhood on the dusty edge of Old Buckhead Road and that Christmas and birthdays knit all of us into time and family.

The frame house we rented was itself nothing special. Built in 1911, the structure shuddered when winter winds rushed beneath it, turning floor boards bitterly cold. We huddled around a brown oil heater on the coldest days, wearing socks on socks, watching the flickering image of a small black-and-white television set. Like many southern houses of its era, it had a shotgun hallway to catch the breeze, but about 1958, we partitioned it, creating a new room next to my parents' bedroom, where my brother Mark and I slept in the winter. A dour carpenter with a cigarette dangling from his thin lips had recently underpinned the house, and I watched him with interest while he watched me with suspicion.

And yet that house has endured in family history, even myth. Except for my sister Laura Jane, who was too young to remember much of it, all of us dreamed about what we called "the old house" for years. Even well into my thirties, I would find myself, in the shifting debris of dreams, standing in the front room, motes streaming through the windows and floating on the summer light like honey suspended in a jar. No one else ever joined me in that enduring dream silence. I felt a closeness and love in that house I found nowhere else, and I am certain those feelings were born of a happy childhood. The house, then, was nothing special, a structure of white wooden siding with two sentinel water oaks in the front yard and a chinaberry tree dangling its shriveled fruits at the end of the front porch.

A field awash in broom sedge lay across the road. Behind the house and to one side a pleasant pasture spread, where cows owned by the county prison farm grazed passively, and we boys played endless games of baseball, pitching and hitting until the sky slid into darkness on the wings of lightning bugs. On the left was a fallow piece of ground sloping down to a swift and deep-sided creek, which was no more than four feet across. Up the slope across that creek a sprawling structure called the Teacherage squatted, built as a girls' dorm back when the high school had been an A & M institution decades before. A group of high school teachers and their families lived there. Butch Huff and Jimmy Williamson were my closest friends, though both were older. Morgan County High School was just beyond the Teacherage, a cluster of red-brick structures. The Administration Building was its center piece, with four white columns holding up the front portico.

But what really kept my attention, shaped me with a pleasant permanence, was the forest. Just beyond the pasture, directly behind our house and only a few hundred yards distant, the pine woods began. I loved the grandeur of a hardwood forest, with its oak canopy and hickories that drop their nuts to a mossy bed with a pleasant thunk. Far more than oaks, I loved the sweet resin of pine and cedar, the feel of needles beneath my shoes. More than once I arrived home at dusk with pine tar black and gummy on my hands from touching the dripped sap and bringing it to my nose.

Those woods held more than trees, though. Rocks were exposed there millions of years before, shelves and slabs of granite near which we camped. I dreamed of being Daniel Boone as I scrambled up the largest ones, seeing the glories of a new continent for the first time. Farther into the pines a bold creek meandered past, a stream whose bottom held a bed of those same stones, and we boys called it Rocky Island, though it was not an island at all, just one lovely glen far enough from any road to anchor our private hours. A treasure was buried not far from Rocky Island. When a drug store in Madison burned years before, they had brought the debris there and covered it with rich soil, and from time to time, cream pitchers, pieces of crockery, halves of white coffee cups would work their way up into the filtered light.

My very first memory of that land was not of cracked crockery, however, but of mica. For decades I have held this scene in my memory:

I am walking with my father, and we come through a forest whose trees seem to rake the sky. I am very small, perhaps four or five, and we are in a clearing, the grass is cattle-gnawed, and before us the ground dips and swells. Suddenly, my father reaches down and lifts up a great sheet of mica, bigger than his hand, and the sun catches it and shoots a dazzling beam into my eyes. I am reaching out to touch that light when the scene evaporates.

Perhaps that walk combines memory and invention, though I can never be sure. My father's strong hand held me safely, offered myth, as if we found the Rhine gold or stumbled into pictures from a fairy tale. On good nights, it still comes back in my dreams, and I am small again, amazed to see a sheet of mica as large as my own father's hand.

three

Not long after we moved to Madison, I awoke to a sensate world in the country. Christmas was among my earliest memories, but I longed to explore the world beyond the safety of my mother's arms, too. And so I discovered animals in that simple world.

The hen house, behind our home and huddled next to the pasture fence, was warm and fecund. We kept layers for their eggs, though sometimes my mother would kill one of them for a Sunday meal. I still recall with distaste the killing scenes, the hatchet rising and falling with a thud and the bloody death. My mother had grown up in a small mill town in South Carolina, but even this was new for her. The taste of her fried chicken was heavenly, but the killing, plucking, and cleaning were ghastly to me. I never got used to it.

The hen house was a different matter, for I have never minded farm smells and in truth rather like them. My first memory of the hen house: stealing alone inside one dusty afternoon and lifting a hen off her nest to find a single perfect egg. I took it outside into the brighter light and held it aloft, and it was beautiful, the shell like glass, highly polished and slick. I adored it, pressed it in my palms lightly and then to my cheeks. Then I ducked inside, returned the egg to the yeasty nest and fled. Later that evening when I told my father of the egg, he smiled and revealed the secret: it did not only feel like glass; it *was* glass, an elegant ruse to keep hens on the nest and laying. I felt mildly foolish, but after that I would sneak in with the hens and look for the fabulous glass eggs and feel their texture, warm them in my small palms.

One of my earliest and most enduring memories is of gathering eggs while my father sat on the back porch reading Wordsworth's magnificent "Lines Composed A Few Miles Above Tintern Abbey" out loud. Once, when I'd been sent out alone to get eggs, I gathered too many, and as I came back up the back steps I dropped one and watched in horror as it tumbled from my hands and splattered, dripping yolk and white through the sagging slat. I wept in fear and frustration, but my mother only scolded me lightly.

Earlier in 1959, the hen house was in such bad condition that my father pulled it down entirely. We quit keeping chickens, and I was secretly glad we would kill no more of them, even though I missed going to collect the eggs. I gauged that world by small changes, the only kind I had ever known.

four

Christmas was all charm in the 1950s. In those idle days, a boy could still be pleased with oranges, Brazil nuts, and a few special toys. Before Christmas 1959, my most memorable gifts had been a matched set of Roy Rogers pistols with leather holsters, cowboy boots, a basketball, and some tinker toys. The pebbled texture on the metal handles of my six-shooters was lovely, and I played with them for years before they finally disappeared. Toy makers had not yet discovered how to construct cheap, light-metal knock-offs in the early 1950s, so the guns were heavy and solid, and yet completely unreal. I could not, even then, bear to hurt any living thing, but those pistols were only for a kind of ritualized movie envy.

Santa brought me the magnificent gift of a Lionel Army train in 1958, olive drab, with a rocket-launcher car. I felt a quiet pride in the military theme, because our parents had saved the Earth in World War II. (I was born just as the Korean conflict was heating up, but few people ever mentioned it.) Both my parents had been in the military, my father in the Army Air Force, stationed in England, and my mother in the Navy's WAVE program, with postings first in New York and later in San Francisco. If we boys were not playing baseball or pretending to be cowboys, we were soldiers in those sunny fields, attacking German gun emplacements, daring to peek over the top of trenches toward death with the kind of bravery only children can show.

But greater than any of these games was football. That fall the Morgan County Bulldogs had torn through their Region 4-B schedule, hoping to win the state championship for the fourth time in the past five years, the team led by a hard-driving and brilliant coach named Bill Corry. My father had recommended that the school board hire him in 1955 when our first championship coach, Charlie Brake, left for another school. Coach Corry had never played high school football, and one school board member opposed his hiring, but Corry's sheer hard work and native intelligence had won over all the skeptics virtually from the beginning. The 1959 team, Corry would remember in later years, had a nearly awesome balance and determination. Since my father was principal, I virtually grew up on the sidelines, and my respect for the coaches and players was tinged with awe.

On Saturday mornings I would often take my old leather football to the high school field (only a few hundred yards from our house) and practice field goals from a muddy divot I made with my heel. Since I was barefoot almost all the time when the weather was not freezing cold, I learned to kick shoeless, and in time it felt as natural as anything I've ever done. I would stand in that early morning stillness, quite alone, the programs and popcorn from the game still littering the stands as if there had been a ticker-tape parade. I would imagine time running out, then a clean snap of the ball, and my foot swinging down, then up, in a sweet arc. And the ball, a cast-off whose rubber bladder showed on the ends from beneath the worn leather, would leap upward in a perfect end-over-end tumble, rising and rising until it spun between the uprights, and I lifted both arms in triumph.

That silent crowd in my imagination went mad. My teammates lifted me on their padded shoulders as I was borne from that victory field in glory. Or, if I missed, there would be a penalty on the defense, and I would have another chance to make the field goal. I might kick for hours, the sound of my bare foot making a flat thwack against the ball. I worked on punting, but I was far less good at it. At other times I would simply start running down the field, stiff-arming my opponents, running in that rising sun until I was in the end zone, breathless and exultant. The only sound was the wind. From the east end zone I could even see our house past the Teacherage, across the creek, nesting in the shade of its oaks.

I didn't always play football alone. Even though we lived in the edge of the country and I had free run of the high school field, we often played in town or north of Madison in the front yard of my friend Wayne Tamplin. When I ran in the silence of the high school stadium, I was invincible, swift, courageous. When I played with my friends, I was slow, awkward, and easily knocked off my feet. (While wearing a broken helmet from the high school team, I had my two top front baby teeth knocked out of my head a couple of years earlier in the front yard of Jack Lindsey, who lived on the other side of the high school. His father was, for years, the only veterinarian in the county.) My uniform in those days was put together from old pieces I got from the high school or bartered from friends. What I wanted was a red uniform, Morgan County High School Bulldog red, so that I could stand against an enemy the way my beloved high school team did.

I felt in those days as if we could lose nothing—wars or football games. I was sure that our settled life in the country would go on for years to come, that I would grow into my role as the barefooted kicker who won games and was brought into honor by the shouts of the fans and my adoring team.

five

That blessed safety was rocked the year before. At the age of forty-three, my uncle, Vincent Astor Williams, whom everybody called Sambo, died suddenly. He was my father's older brother, the second of his siblings to die. (Another brother, Cecil, had died tragically in 1944.) Worse, my father's parents were dead, too, the grandparents I never knew. I was somewhat afraid of Sambo because he was bluff and loud and sometimes used colorful language, the kind you never heard in my house, but he was also more full of life than virtually anybody I ever knew. The summer before he died, I stayed with him and my Aunt "Mac" at their home near Seneca, South Carolina, and Sambo let me shoot his .22 rifle and .38 pistol, both of which frightened me and made me feel grown up.

Now he was gone into memory. I tried not to think of him, but I had lost something that September 1958, a certainty that I would never have again. Still, my own family could hardly have been more stable. The following year, we had a new baby, and I was having to adjust to that, but we all adored Laura Jane, and she was bright and funny as she grew. I was also, for the first time, beginning to understand the passions of literature and music that drove my parents. Mother was a lover of opera, and the sounds of the Saturday Metropolitan Opera broadcasts filtered through the house. My father loved orchestral music more, and we had a large collection of 78 rpm albums, including one gargantuan set of Handel's *Messiah*.

That December 1, Winston Churchill turned eighty-five. President Eisenhower left on a visit to many countries to sell America and peace. A popular television show was "The Many Loves of Dobie Gillis." The TV column in *The Atlanta Constitution* said that night's episode would be amusing, and that "Warren Beatty, Shirley MacLaine's brother, plays the lad making the fast exit."

Mother says I taught myself to read before I went to the first grade, and I loved the newspaper, read it passionately, trying to make sense of the news. We understood the danger of nuclear war, though I could not believe anyone would bomb us on Old Buckhead Road. A few years later, during the height of the Cuban Missile Crisis, I recall a friend saying, "If I don't wake up tomorrow morning, I'm going to be really mad." I started laughing then stopped. How should a child feel in the face of such horrors?

Georgia's Civil Defense leaders tried to whip the state into a frenzy that autumn over the threat of Soviet attack. For several years, Atlanta had an evacuation plan in case of nuclear war. Jack Grantham, deputy director of state Civil Defense said this: "In the event a nuclear bomb were dropped on Lockheed Aircraft Corporation, mass evacuation of Metropolitan Atlanta would be feasible only if we have three-to-four hours' warning."

Another front-page headline from December 1959: 100 Cities Are Trying Malls; Should Atlanta Join Them?

Vivien Leigh's marriage to Laurence Oliver was reported to be in trouble. The U. S. on December 2 launched a space monkey named Sam atop a "Little Joe" rocket from Wallop Island, off the eastern shore of Virginia. Sam went up fifty-five miles and came down safely. His picture was on front pages all over America, a now-forgotten space pioneer. In an ad for his Pickrick restaurant in Atlanta, Lester Maddox wrote, "I sure hope the integrationists don't close our schools." Billy Cannon of Louisiana State University won what was then called the Heisman "Cup." A Lionel steam freight model train with five cars was advertised for $29.95, a fortune.

What I read most, though, had nothing to do with war or peace or the private lives of the famous. I read the funny papers. Many of those old strips have long since faded with the writers and artists who created them, but a startling number still appear. I loved Peanuts, Beetle Bailey, B. C., Dick Tracy, Steve Canyon, Pogo, and They'll Do It Every Time. I even read the soaps like Mary Worth. My favorite was The Phantom—The Ghost Who Walks. I stayed tangled in his jungle adventures for months on end, loved him almost as much as Tarzan. We had a new Tarzan at the movies that year, Gordon Scott, and I wanted to swing in trees, tell mysterious truths, command wild beasts with my voice.

The printed material we boys loved most was not a newspaper, though. The Sears Christmas Catalog was our *War and Peace*, the place where Christmas really lived. I lay on my stomach and pored over its pages for hours, folding back the corners on gifts I could request and those I knew we could not possibly afford. My favorites when I was smaller were the farm scenes—hundreds of plastic pieces, squat hogs, cows with white faces, fence rails, barns, tractors, horses. I set them up in the dirt and played with them for hours.

We also loved the small green army men, and Mark and I arranged them for hours in the red-clay ditch in front of our house. My mother recalls one Christmas eve when it was very warm, and we boys spent the entire day playing with army men, setting up battles, arranging assaults, flanking the enemy. I thought this was something new, and I did not discover until years later that one of my favorite composers, Johannes Brahms, spent much of his childhood in the 1830s and 1840s playing with lead soldiers just as I played with the plastic kind. The Sears Christmas Catalog had plenty of army sets, and I read the fine print, the exciting descriptions, and dreamed of finding them under our cedar tree Christmas morning.

I knew that warm early December what I wanted, though. I had plenty of army men by then, and plastic farm animals turned up everywhere. I owned a second-hand bicycle and rode it for miles on the newly paved road in front of our house. (Old Buckhead Road was a red ribbon of dust when we moved there in 1953 and stayed unpaved for several years. I never liked it as much paved as I did raw and bare, though my mother was glad for the red dust to disappear with the paving.) What I wanted was a football uniform.

I could hardly think of anything but football, since the Bulldogs were traveling to the west Georgia town of Villa Rica to play for the North Georgia Class B title on the night of December 5. We had won twenty-three straight games, and I could not bear losing. I was neither strong nor fast, but I hoped some day I would be a star on that team. Life offered no higher honors.

If I had my own red football uniform, I could begin that preparation. I could be an acolyte at the altar of the strong and fast.

six

Children want to be like their friends, so to be different is agony. And yet in one respect I was very different: None of our relatives lived anywhere near Madison, not even in Georgia. My parents were South Carolinians from that state's Oconee County, snug in the northwest corner of the state where the Piedmont turns into foothills. Every Christmas morning, after we opened our presents and played with the bounty from Santa Claus, we piled in our car, a cream-over-turquoise 1956 Chevrolet, and headed north on U. S. 441 for the two-hour drive to Seneca. Since my father's parents were dead (he lost his mother in 1947, his father in 1935) we chiefly visited my mother's parents, Lillie and Lee Sisk, who lived in a cozy two-story house on shady South Fourth Street in Seneca. Since we did not have to distinguish between two sets of grandparents as most of my friends did, we called them the same thing Mother did: Mama and Papa.

I loved Papa and Mama. His hair had begun to turn gray, though it was red in his youth, and when he laughed his belly would rise and fall over his narrow black belt. He worked in the company store at Courtney Mills, a textile plant in the small nearby town of Newry. Mother was born in Newry, though the family moved to Seneca in 1939. Papa loved his customers, sold the world's best ground beef, told endless stories. He kept up with baseball and sometimes followed the St. Louis Cardinals. He and my grandmother had for years lived in separate bedrooms, and at night during the summer I slept in his room, Papa on his single bed and sometimes just me on a sagging double bed with a painted, decorative iron frame. We listened to baseball games in the darkness of his room while insects banged into the screen, coming toward the faint light from the front of his General Electric radio. He could sit quietly for an hour working on a crossword puzzle.

Papa always wore a hat outdoors, straw in the summer and felt in the winter, part of the last generation to do so. My mother and father raised us to travel in fear of cliches and improper use of language, but Lee Sisk "never met a stranger," and that old phrase describes him as well as anything else.

Mama made the best fried chicken I ever ate. She was quiet, calm, and plump, and she smiled frequently. Her father had been the chief mechanic at the mill—an "inventor" she would say proudly. She had blue eyes. We found out years later from census records that she listed as being two years older than my grandfather, but she would never discuss her age. She always said they were born the same year—1898. Her house was filled with treasured knickknacks. She loved to sit at the table after supper and talk with her children and grandchildren about this small world and the larger one, too.

Mark and I always slept upstairs in the winter, an unheated, thinly insulated space with windows that swung back horizontally because of the low ceilings. When I came up the narrow, hollow-sounding stairs into that quietness, I felt a genuine peace, fringed with a vague uneasiness. The two bedrooms teemed with secret places, holes in the wall through which you could hide boxes, a storage area created with a curtain in the central room that joined the two bedrooms. I always looked into the guardian chifferobe, full of my uncles' collections: arrowheads, unusual stones, photographs, old clothes. There were also old books, Papa's ancient shotgun, and issues of the *National Geographic* going back at least to 1919.

My Uncle Mike, my mother's baby brother, was only eighteen that year and a freshman at Furman University in Greenville, S.C. He had been Seneca High School's valedictorian and would later become a pediatric neurologist. (In my generation, I never had much hope to be a superior student for I daydreamed too often, but my sister Laura Jane would go on to be valedictorian of Morgan County High School in 1977.) Mike and Mark and I were more like brothers than uncle and nephews, and his obvious brilliance rubbed off on us both. I suppose Mike was home that Christmas, but I cannot remember it. I only know that in winter we slept in narrow single beds in those upstairs rooms with the low ceilings. We dreamed beneath layer after layer of homemade quilts, motionless until body heat filled the space between our small bodies and the cotton-stuffed mattresses. We listened to the trains as they came through town, a few blocks away.

One winter night at Mama's house, I awoke to find myself trembling from the cold. The ambient light from a street lamp in the front yard on South Fourth Street always meant a dim glow came through, but on this night, a full moon lay upon the surface of the window, too.

Downstairs: the comforting laughter of adults. In the other bed: my brother asleep, his body rising and falling beneath four quilts. I went fetal, tried to hold what little heat I generated, but I could not stop trembling, so I crawled from beneath the covers and sat on the edge of the bed, saw my breath in moonlight, decided to creep down the stairs until I felt some of the warmth from below.

I walked on my hard bare feet across the splintery floorboards and suddenly felt, in my cheeks, a wisp of heat. A chimney rose directly through the middle of the room from the dining room fireplace like a brick pyre. Mama kept that fireplace going all winter with coal in its cradling grate, and from the sounds below I knew the adults were huddled around it, probably drinking coffee and homemade hot chocolate while spinning tales. The heat I felt came from the chimney bricks. I got closer, the room unnaturally bright from the moon and full of shadows. My own shadow stretched from the window to the chimney, past which darkness gathered, and I felt the warmth growing stronger and stronger.

I came to the chimney and leaned slowly toward it, because I did not want to awaken Mark, and I pressed my shivering cheek to the bricks, and a delicious warmth flooded me. I spread myself against them, cruciform, feeling the steady heat from that tarry smoke as it rose into the quiet, cold night. As I did, the voices came strongly again from downstairs, and I felt suddenly as if nothing could harm me ever and that this heat rose for me alone.

I stayed there until I was drowsy and then slid back into bed where I immediately fell asleep until I was awakened the next morning by the smell of coffee rising up the narrow stairs. For years after that in winter, I would rise in the light of the moon, even on rainy nights when I could see almost nothing, and I would tiptoe to the chimney and press my face against it and feel the flush of life below me and the warmth of those bricks upon my small cheek.

seven

My mother's family at Christmas time was easy. I had two grandparents, my Uncle Mike, and my Uncle Charles and his family all living in Seneca. Aunt Laura, my mother's sister, lived with her family in Rock Hill, South Carolina, about as far away from Seneca as Madison. I did not know my mother's eldest brother Harmon very well, since he lived in New York State and only came south occasionally. Despite the fact that my father's parents were dead, the lines of his family were more tangled in Oconee County than Mother's. Because his father and two other Williams brothers married three Jaynes sisters, the county was teeming with aunts, uncles, and cousins. In addition, there were great aunts and uncles.

One of my favorites was Aunt Sally Duncan, who lived a block farther toward town than Mama and Papa. She was actually my great-aunt and was born on Bastille Day, July 14, in 1877, so by that Christmas of 1959 she was eighty-two, yet would live another nine years. Aunt Sally had a voice like a squeaky screen door, and sometimes her gaze would light on something as if she were seeing it for the first time. Then, she would stare at it almost in disgust, touch it, and shrug. Later, she would dream up colorful notions involving conspiracy theories and J. Edgar Hoover, but for the most part she loved to recall the distant past, and my father talked to her about those years for hours on end. She could retell how her big brother John, just a boy of fourteen, had been killed on Christmas Day 1888 when a tree limb fell on him. He had been out squirrel hunting. Christmas Day was freighted ever after with those terrible memories, but she didn't mind recalling them or anything else. After all, it had been seventy-one years in the past. Aunt Sally was my Grandfather Williams's sister—in all, there were 10 Williams brothers and sisters. Equally entangling, my father's mother had eight brothers and sisters. Relatives lived everywhere in that part of the state.

The person we visited the most by far, however, was my father's sister, Vivian Crenshaw, known by all as "Ben," because one of her brothers couldn't pronounce her name when they were children. Aunt Ben and her husband Chris had two sons, Arthur and Bob. Arthur was the same age as my Uncle Mike and his friend, while Bob was a year older than Mark.

Aunt Ben had turned forty-seven that September and seemed much younger than Uncle Chris, who was silver-haired and had sharp features that came out in Arthur's face. Chris held one endless fascination for us: he collected stamps. Mark and I had begun, probably in 1958, to order packets of stamps from the H. E. Harris Company in Boston. Uncle Chris had a stunning stamp collection that I envied—plate blocks, Confederate stamps, early commemoratives. I would sit for hours studying his collection as he patiently told their stories and sipped on a cigarette.

Aunt Ben was, I think, the happiest person I ever knew. She was always glad to see us, and the ritual of visiting

Seneca, especially at Christmas, included a stop at her house on Walnut Street before we turned south back toward Georgia and Madison. She cooked a full meal if anybody seemed vaguely hungry, including fluffy biscuits and delicious fried meat. Her small refrigerator in the kitchen always held a store of six-ounce Cokes, standing like soldiers in formation. She was smart and musical, and often laughed until she was helpless with tears. Her house was the same one in which my father grew up, the same home where his father had died in 1935. For me, the place was equally full of fond memories and ghosts, and I always felt a slight discomfort as the youngest cousin, but Aunt Ben never tired of hugging me or asking me of my child's life. She listened with an obvious passion because she cared far more about others than herself.

The Christmas tree I always recall from Aunt Ben's house was an artificial tree of bright silver—the first one I had ever seen. Along with it was a rotating color disc on the floor from whose light the branches turned green, yellow, or red. Perhaps this tree was from later years, but I remember it with affection nonetheless.

We always came home exhausted and happy after Christmas, with a few days left to play before we headed back to school. On the warmer Saturdays in winter, Mark and I still headed for the deep woods, carrying some prize from Santa Claus into the larger world we understood better than any other.

And so, every Christmas, we set out for Seneca from Madison, hoarding the few toys my mother let us bring, knowing that more awaited from the houses on South Fourth and Walnut streets. I never spent a full Christmas Day at home during all my childhood years, but I could imagine no holiday more beautiful than those I spent near that welcoming hearth in South Carolina.

eight

We were religious people, and we went to the First Baptist Church every Sunday morning, every Sunday night, most Wednesday evenings. I could not wait each year to hear the first reading of the Christmas story: *And there went out a decree from Caesar Augustus that all the world should be taxed.* The image of the Christ child moved me deeply, and I was more sure with each passing year that I deserved neither his love nor his grace.

Slaves built our church in 1858, and according to one story, greatly amplified over a century, Union soldiers stabled their horses in the basement when they briefly came through during General William T. Sherman's March to the Sea in 1864. (Sherman himself did not come through town.) The sanctuary was the standard vault with magnificent stained-glass windows that I spent hours studying when I was ignoring the sermons. The gallery in the rear, where the slaves of rich planters sat during services until war came, was by the late 1950s beloved of the older boys, a place for mild misbehavior. There were no pews up there, just ladder-back chairs, and when I sat downstairs in the back of the sanctuary with my family, I could hear the boys up there, scraping chair legs and giggling.

From the beginning, I felt safe and happy in church. I did not question theology until years later, going straight from faith to agnosticism in a wrenching jolt—hitting that wall at a near-lethal speed. The slow journey back to faith from doubt was also a long one and one of the most difficult transitions of my life. But in 1959, I had few questions about religion, and its comfort reassured me. I was no more devout than the next nine-year-old; however, my dreaminess, my tendency to go off on tangents of dazzling music and the spoken word, kept me open-mouthed rather than prayerful during most of my church hours. First Baptist was a large in-town church, and our creed was simple, our faith strong.

The story of the crucifixion always saddened me. I understood sacrifice, but I could not understand a man brutally stretched upon a cross, bleeding and dying in the name of religion. I could not imagine that day when the curtain in the temple tore, and a vast thunderstorm broke as Jesus died. I knew thunderstorms well enough and rather enjoyed them as Mark and I sat on the covered, wrap-around front porch of our house in the country and played games, staring at the harp-string strands of rain. Sometimes, missing the sermon altogether, I stared at the crucifixion in the stained glass window and wondered how much He suffered and why it happened. I shuddered, realizing the sermon had ended and I had heard none of it at all. More often, I drew pictures of battleships on the back of the church bulletin, deck on deck, guns blazing at the enemy. My father, who knew radio and television design as well as he knew anything, would sit next to me and sometimes draw electronic diagrams, with sequences of tubes and resistors.

Christmas was my favorite part of the church year, as it was for all nine-year-olds. It had the lovely songs such as "It Came Upon the Midnight Clear" and "Silent Night." My father's passionate love of music did not extend to singing—I never once heard him sing in church or anywhere else. But Mother sang beautifully and sat in the choir off and on for many years, at least explaining why she loved opera and Daddy preferred orchestral music. (All the Williams children turned out to be musical, Mark as a guitarist and Laura Jane as a superb pianist. I became a composer, singer, and mediocre keyboard player.)

That Christmas season, I found it easy to be grateful. The Morgan County Bulldogs had roared through the regular season undefeated. They would play for the North Georgia title on December 5, the big, strong boys banging in their red uniforms, me on the sidelines daydreaming myself into their shoes. We also had a new baby in the family, and I enjoyed watching her change day by day, though she would still be only a day over three months old on Christmas Day. There were no major conflicts abroad. As usual, Mark was better that summer at Little League than I was, but that was the nature of things. I had begun to notice the other sex and had my eye on a pretty, fresh-faced young girl named Faye Harwell, though it would take me another year to hold her hand in the darkness of the Madison Theatre during a screening of *Gone with the Wind*. The community respected my mother and father, though sometimes Daddy's poorer students were wary of him.

A perfect order cradled my life. I was entirely happy. The Christmas season at church was filled with the kind of eggnog good will that is easy to deride and which some people spend the rest of their lives trying to duplicate. There was only one problem. I had not yet "joined the church" because I was terrified of walking down the aisle and standing before several hundred pairs of staring eyes. I don't think I lacked the creed—that part was easy. I just came up short in courage, and because of it, I was ashamed.

I tried not to think of it, though, and so I rolled through the early Christmas season singing the familiar hymns and thinking of a baby born in the warm safety of a barn.

nine

Southerners love the spoken word at Christmas as much as they love family and rich food. Our deepest traditions are more oral than written, and everyone from preachers to old aunts open the book of memory and retell the stories of Christmases from many years before. Many of my South Carolina relatives were born long before automobiles and electricity in homes, and they never tired of relating to a small boy what life was like back then.

Without exception, each of them liked Christmas better in those languid days of the late nineteenth and early twentieth centuries, but each of them could speak for hours with the kind of passion for talking not uncommon in the days before radio.

My father loved also to read out loud. One of my earliest memories is the sound of his sonorous voice reading poetry and short stories. Edgar Allen Poe thrilled me, Robert W. Service made me laugh, and the Biblical Christmas story never failed to move me. Daddy had been in England during the war, so when he read any of the Lake Country poets, he infused their words with memories of his own.

From that love of words, it was a short trip to books. We read all the time, everybody in the house. Mark and I subscribed to *Boy's Life*, the magazine of Scouting, but I also read anything else I could find. Mother read constantly, too, though her time was much taken with Laura Jane as that Christmas approached. I also skimmed *The Atlanta Journal* and *The Madisonian* and lay on my stomach reading, especially the sports section.

My father's favorite form of writing, hands down, was poetry. He had written some very good verse himself as a young man, though by 1959 he wrote very little. (When President Kennedy was assassinated four years later, he would send one of his poems of consolation to Mrs. Kennedy and received a black-bordered, form thank-you note. I am sure that thousands received the same card, but to me it might have been the Pulitzer—a thank you from the widow of our slain president.) I admired the precision and regularity of normal verse, but Daddy also had a few books that were filled with modern poetry—T. S. Eliot, Wallace Stevens, and many others now forgotten. Among the most startling poems to me was "Peter Quince at the Clavier" by Stevens. Though Daddy seldom read the "moderns" out loud (except for Vachel Lindsay), I was already secretly staring at the words on the page, trying to tease out meaning, failing. And yet they were so seductive. A poem like "The Hollow Men" left me feeling strangely dislocated and curious.

I knew from the Bible that words had power. The Christmas story always left me frustrated at the stupidity of the innkeeper, then exalted by the arrival of the wise men to worship the baby. I also adored the Psalms, with their breast-beating and wailing and hosannas. But above all I admired the

32
✳

quieter books of poetry, not the thunder of prophecy or the terrible beauty of the gospels.

There was a rich world of words beyond the Bible, though, and I had just begun to discover it that year. Arthur Conan Doyle was a family hero, but above all my father's favorite poet at that time was William Wordsworth, who supremely caught the rhythms of happiness in the natural world, regret, love, and exaltation. Daddy was forever bursting into Wordsworth, blossoming with wild rills and rocks and cascades and other lovely words.

When I was in the third grade, my wonderful teacher, Mrs. Frances Biggers, asked us what we wanted to be when we grew up—she wished to see how many wound up in a profession first dreamed as an eight-year-old. I knew immediately, didn't have to think about it: "I want to be in the artillery, in the Army," I blurted. She dutifully wrote it down. Then we went to lunch.

In 1957 a new elementary school opened a few hundred yards from our house on Old Buckhead Road, so I walked, alone, across the broad broom sedge field from it to our house each noon for the delicious lunch Mother cooked for me. In the spring, I always arrived with a small fistful of wildflowers for my best friend, and she would feign surprise and show genuine delight. I ate, stretched, played with the cat, and then walked back to school, waving my hands across the top of the broom sedge and humming drowsily.

At lunch that day, I had a change of heart about my profession. Being in the artillery was probably a good idea, since I could be a hero like all my friends' fathers, but I kept hearing my father speaking about something called archaeology. We had found Indian artifacts on the land and even discovered a site rich with pottery and arrowheads back near the woods. Already, we had begun to collect things systematically and would eventually turn it all over to the University of Georgia. But archaeology really meant one thing: Tutankhamen. In more than one book, I had seen the pictures of the boy king's gold mask, and my father had read aloud the story of Howard Carter finding that stunning site in the Valley of the Kings. (Oddly enough for me, that discovery had come two weeks after my father's birth in 1922.)

So, when I got back, I took Mrs. Biggers aside and asked gravely if it were possible to add one other possible profession to my prediction. I was genuinely worried that she would say no, that I would have no choice other than firing big guns in the next war. She smiled at me and said, "Of course you can." I almost whispered, "I also want to be an archaeologist." I don't recall her reaction, but it probably wasn't the normal third-grade aspiration in Madison in 1958. Years later, there was a movie about archaeology set during the time of war—*Raiders of the Lost Ark*—and I remember thinking this was the perfect place for my third grade self. I would not become an archaeologist, but my brother Mark would.

It wasn't until well into the 1960s that I began to think back on the marvelous words that my mother and father read to us, a partially multilingual world. My parents were both college graduates, and Daddy had mastered German and would hurry us up by shouting *Macht schnell!* Mother loved the cadences of Latin and Italian—being an opera lover, what else would it be? Her favorite aria was not one of the great dramatic set pieces but *"O Mio Babino Caro,"* the tender song from Puccini's small opera *Gianni Schicci*.

What would I be? A composer. That came to me in my early teens, and I have never given up on that great ambition.

But I could not deny the influence of words. By my mid-teens I knew that I would be, in some measure, a writer, and that my life would always be turning back to that house in the country where the woods and the fields opened before me and lured me into such a lasting and bright solitude.

✳

ten

Though my relatives all lived a hundred miles distant, I was held close by my own family as that Christmas season came close in 1959. I thought I had been good, but a boy could never be entirely sure. The warm weather of autumn disappeared and cold fronts slid beneath us in a lordly succession. I read constantly and my father read poetry aloud, and Mother rocked Laura Jane by the oil heater on the colder days.

Some Saturdays I rode my bike a mile to the Rock Store, a gas station out on U.S. 441, to buy a Nehi grape drink or some "sand crackers," small explosives pellets that gave a sharp report when thrown against a wall or floor. The store was actually covered with huge chunks of white and yellow quartz, cemented into the front of the building and the twin pillars that held a porch out to the gas pumps. Or I might pedal the other direction out Old Buckhead Road, deep into the country, perhaps to an Indian site we had lately discovered. I came home late, pockets bulging and heavy with pottery sherds and arrowheads.

Mostly, I played football with my friends or by myself, and waited without much patience for the state playoffs. I would not be able to enjoy Christmas until that magnificent trophy shone behind glass in a hallway at the high school.

The Bulldogs began that autumn by edging Newton County 7-0, one of six shutouts our defense posted in 10 regular-season games. During one stretch in mid-season, we slammed Georgia Military College, Jefferson, Oglethorpe County, and Monticello by scores of 47-0, 40-0, 53-0, and 20-0. As usual, the toughest game of the year was against our arch-rival, Washington-Wilkes, but we beat them 13-12, leaving me exhausted but elated. Perhaps somewhat let down the week after that contest, we defeated Hart County only 20-13.

The post-season began on November 20 when we easily bested Tallulah Falls, 41-20. On November 27, the Bulldogs took the Region 4-B title by shutting out Rockdale County 27-0. So we were ready on a cold December night to play Villa Rica for the North Georgia Class B title. I was miserable with fear for the team. I barely remembered the 1955 state champions, knew the 1956 champs only vaguely. By 1958, however, I was eight years old and the principal's kid, and so I had begun to hang around games, prowling the sidelines, watching the games from touching distance. Now, in 1959, I was old enough to know that I was somehow part of the team.

The whole town was football mad. The players were much smaller in those days, and the paper even called one of our backs, Ray Bennett, "Morgan's dazzling 138-pound flash." Charles Ruark was bigger at 150, and Bonar Newton and Neal Vason were even more impressive. Our quarterback Bobby Tamplin held the team together.

Eight buses were chartered to take my townsmen to the small west Georgia town of Bremen, a neutral field. Everyone worried about Villa Rica because they had two backs who had gained more than 1,300 yards each that season. Still, we had not lost a game since a 6-0 contest with Covington in the autumn of 1958, and Villa Rica was 10-0-1 that year, and that tie was an unpardonable blemish in my eyes. Even the announcement that week that the Santa Claus would visit Madison arriving on "our fire truck" (as the paper said) later in the month didn't excite me much.

I had a pair of real football shoes. They were cracked, torn, and cast off from the team, but their long, tripping cleats were perfect, and I could keep them on my feet if I walked slowly. So there I was, every day after school that week, clown-footed, flapping in the side yard trying to kick my old football and dreaming of winning the game. It would take some growing, but one day I'd fit them. My football could rupture any moment, and I was wary, but when I approached the ball, all I envisioned was the ball rising and rising in a tumbling arc, then falling through the goal posts. In those days, kicking was a delicate art, and only a few high schools kicked extra points; most still lined up and tried to pound it in. I kicked and kicked with those clumsy shoes and found that I was terrible, and so I pulled them off in the cold grass and kicked barefooted, watching the ball go farther than I ever thought it could.

The night of the game against Villa Rica I was numb with excitement. I had never heard such noise. When the players ran on to the field, they were leaping, piling on each other, and I thought they could rise to heaven if they merely raised their strong arms. We had gone to the game as usual on the band buses, and the band members chanted *Beat Beat Beat Beat VILLA Rica VILLA Rica* over and over.

Villa Rica kicked off to us—a very short kick, and I was immediately contemptuous. Shoot, I thought, I can kick farther than that. Neal Vason immediately began driving up the middle behind our strong offensive line, and when we got to the Villa Rica twenty, Bobby Tamplin faked up the middle and threw Branham Garth a touchdown pass. Villa Rica, however, scored just before the half. Our defense at that point locked the game down, and a nineteen-yard Bonar Newton run in the third quarter made it 14-6. We won for the twenty-fifth straight game! I was delirious, and now only the winner of the Perry-Brooks County game for the South Georgia Class B title stood in our way. I felt as if my feet would never touch the ground as we walked back toward the bus when the game ended.

Children know only glimpses of their parents' world, however, and that December my father's world was changing. He was considering a decision that would alter our lives, but Mark and I never suspected it, never knew how tenuous our grasp on that world had become.

eleven

The week of our victory over Villa Rica, the Chamber of Commerce strung up the Christmas lights downtown, for the second year in a row. They amazed me, cheered my nine-year-old soul. Madison had never had Christmas lights before 1957, though I had seen them passing through Athens on the way to Seneca. Santa Claus would take his regal place on what the paper called a "throne" on the porch of the Courthouse, and Scouts would act as his elves, handing out candy and fruit.

Madison was always neat, the Post Office squatting on the town square with governmental solidity. Decades before, the Courthouse was in the middle of the square, but the county fathers built a new courthouse to replace it on one of the square's corners instead of its center. The old Courthouse later burned and they sold the center of the square to the federal government for a Post Office, in the mind of many a serious mistake.

The town was compact, with everything from the newspaper on one side of the square to a funeral home on the other. Many of the shops and stores had been in the same locations for decades, and change would not accelerate until many years later. Once I walked barefooted to town in the summer and burned my feet so badly on the hot sidewalk that I missed a Little League game.

At one point, the town had three drug stores on the north side of Main Street on the same block, but years earlier, the one farthest north had closed. That did not prevent my townsmen from calling the center one, Madison Drug Store, the "Middle Drug Store" for years and years afterward, to the great confusion of newcomers. Two years before, in 1957, a huge fire blackened one block in downtown Madison, and I did not know about it until we drove to church that Sunday morning. I was staggered; the only thing comparable I had seen were photographs in a history book of bombed-out Europe. Later, I heard tales of one store owner, during the fire, standing in the street and crying, and I could hardly imagine it.

Even more impressive to me in 1957 was the "Panorama of Progress," a celebration of the county's sesquicentennial. All the men in the county grew beards, the women wore bonnets, and kangaroo courts could "arrest" and "fine" a man if his face wasn't bushy enough. Morgan County's history spilled out in a series of vignettes. We had no large stage in town, so the planners took over the most famous venue around: the Morgan County High School football field. A huge play, pretending to show the history of the county since Indian days, sprawled across the grass every night for several days. I was most impressed by a covered wagon and bereft that I couldn't grow whiskers like my father.

The Christmas parade would thrill me. Country boys could be open with their lack of guile in those days.

I loved coming to town to see so many people. I wondered what they did and if any loved writing as much as I did. Another boy did live in town in those years who would be a writer, though we never knew each other. In the December 10 issue of *The Madisonian*, there was a small story about the Cub Scouts visiting a local crafts shop. Buried in the middle of the society pages, the piece did little more than list the names of the scouts and their "mothers."

Halfway through the story, in ten-point type indistinguishable from any others was the name Bobby Harling. He was a couple of years younger than I was, but years later he would become a noted playwright and screenwriter, perhaps best-known for *Steel Magnolias*, the film that made Julia Roberts a star.

One of the "mothers" for the Cubs was his mother, "Mrs. Robert Harling." The family would move long before I knew Bobby, but Madison was home over the years to an amazing number of writers and artists, including Raymond and Benny Andrews. Just twenty miles down the road in Eatonton, a budding author named Alice Walker had come of age. And in Monticello, also not more than twenty-five miles, Trisha Yearwood (years younger than me) would spend her childhood and youth.

And so the Christmas lights brightened our lives, and Santa's throne reminded all children of the coming Christmas. We waited, eyes bright as the closest stars.

twelve

$\text{B}$and instruments of every size and shape drew me to them with an almost sensuous allure. I loved their sounds, their keys, their padded cases. I admired the smell of brass, the unequivocal snap of a snare drum, the piercing insistence of a piccolo.

It would have been easy for a principal to be partial to a football team like ours, and the people of the county might well have expected it. Indeed, many principals in those days were ex-football coaches who had achieved all they wanted on the field. But my father would have none of it. He loved music with a passion that he always made clear to anyone who would listen. And he made sure music was important on the campus.

Since the football season ostensibly ended in November, bands would have plenty of time to rehearse Christmas music for a seasonal concert, but with our football team, we never knew when we'd finish the season. Now December had come, and we were still playing, so the band had to keep marching, keep banging out the fight song.

The Christmas concert for the high school band was also on the night of the parade, an unfortunate scheduling conflict, since they were supposed to perform at the parade. (Organizers would wind up using records and a public address system for the parade.) Our band was superb.

James Williamson was a smiling man with closely cropped hair and a passionate love of band music. When he arrived as director a few years before, the town had just opened its wallets to buy band instruments for the first time. Civic pride meant keeping up with nearby towns, and after World War II high school bands began to flourish. Mr. Williamson, known to everyone as "Uncle Willie," had in short order taught a group of students to play their instruments superbly. The Williamsons lived across the creek from us in the Teacherage, and their oldest son, Jimmy, was my friend, even though he was three years older. We played together, camped together, talked music together. My father listened to classical music and told me some stories of the great composers, but in the Williamson household, music was a living thing, with scores, conducting batons, and instruments seemingly everywhere.

To children, music comes as naturally as breathing. I could not remember a time when music did not fill our house, from our records to Daddy playing hymns on the old upright piano. The Morgan County Band played the first live music I heard outside of church, and that rich sound, heavy with plodding sousaphones, fruity with clarinets, stunned me. I could not imagine such a power as Mr. Williamson wielded in that slim baton. He would raise his arm for attention, then bring it down swiftly—and *music!*

When I could, I hung out around the band room, inhaling the sharp tang of instrument oil, the musty delight of trumpet cases. I would bang the bass drum, dreaming of a special note in the *Symphonie Fantastique* by Hector Berlioz. A teacher named Van Layson (who also lived in the Teacherage with his family) had, I think, a recording of that symphony, and I recall him confiding that the percussionist for one specific bass drum note in his recording played on a *giant* bass drum—perhaps ten feet tall. This was in the days when music-loving neighbors gathered to hear a new recording, especially an LP in those tail-end days of the 78.

The town's pride in its football team spilled over into its band. The point was to out-play, out-march, out-*snappy* the other team's band.

So music and Christmas held me in a singular embrace. Even old people try once again to make that connection with the sentiment of their youths. One elderly lady in our church kept singing in the choir for years until she was ancient, and her vibrato, too wide and wildly variable, could be heard over the entire congregation. Boys made fun of her, and I guess I did, too. At Christmas, though, we tried to stay on decent behavior. Mark and I would lay off some of our fiercer arguments—I always lost anyway, though I did continue to fight the good fight.

If band music had opened to me a world of harmony and counterpoint, then the hymns of Christmas still buoyed me. We always began Christmas music the first Sunday in December:

It came upon the midnight clear, that glorious song of old
Of angels bending near the earth to touch their harps of gold.

Invariably, my father would point out that the words for "I Heard the Bells on Christmas Day" were written by Henry

W. Longfellow or that Felix Mendelssohn composed the music used with the hymn "Hark! The Herald Angels Sing." He expected us to understand the context of the world—how everything fit—and this was only a part of it.

> *O little town of Bethlehem, how still we see thee lie,*
> *Above thy deep and dreamless sleep, the silent stars go by.*

I came to understand that our best hymns have words and music that are insistent—that paint pictures as vivid as stained glass. I could picture that deep sleep and the silent stars going past as the earth revolved majestically beneath them. Who, I wondered, was the author of the words? I knew from the hymnal his name was Phillips Brooks but nothing else. Or the composer, Lewis Redner? They created a part of Christmas that is unforgettable to Christians, and yet they are completely forgotten now.

My favorite was always "Silent Night," perhaps because I understood what a silent night meant. I have heard that silence is unnerving to some city born, but I have always fled to it, not from it. Despite warbling ladies and husky-voweled old men, Christmas hymns always sound beautiful, and that first Sunday in December 1959, they had never sounded more beautiful to a nine-year-old who was sure, somehow, that his favorite football team would not win the state championship.

> *Silent night, holy night, all is calm, all is bright*
> *Round yon Virgin Mother and child!*
> *Holy Infant so tender and mild*
> *Sleep in heavenly peace, sleep in heavenly peace.*

Incredibly, unspeakably, the Williamsons moved to Tennessee earlier that year, and I stood in the road after we had shaken hands and wished them godspeed, watched their car heading north. It seemed quite beyond belief that I would never see Jimmy again or watch Uncle Willie conduct the high school band. Somehow, we had failed him—the town or the high school or somebody.

A large cedar tree rose behind the Teacherage not far from the road, and as the Williamsons left, I climbed up the ladder-limbs very slowly, inhaling the scent of evergreen sap. I was hardly deft, but I managed to get some twenty feet off the ground, thinking I might see the car, but it was long gone by then.

A man named Jack Redwine took over the band, and it sounded fine as ever to me. He would be the one to lead them in their Christmas concert on December 17, not Uncle Willie, and I knew from eavesdropping on rehearsals that it sounded fine as it always did. By then, the football season would be over. And if I had been good enough, a red football uniform might be on its way to me. Of course, I would have very little time to play in it on Christmas morning because we would be heading for South Carolina. I hoped that in between packing and getting the baby ready for travel that I would have time to play outside for a while. If I did, I was sure to be singing, humming, making music.

thirteen

The yearly struggle with Christmas tree lights in our house was a chance both for temper and for instruction, for art and science lived side by side in our house.

My father, who still taught a chemistry class in addition to being principal of the high school, built his own small shop in a room not much bigger than a closet off our back porch. Daddy had been fascinated with radios and chemistry since childhood, and each had an important place in our house. Mark was clearly going to be a scientist of some kind. He built crystal radio sets, experimented with chemicals, took things apart to see how they worked, and then put them back together. I could take things apart, but I was hopeless at restoring them, no matter how simple.

Mother put up with it all with her typical good cheer. She enjoyed keeping house for her ever-expanding brood and for a husband who seemed to be interested in *everything*. Daddy would stop us on a field walk to lecture about natural process, about ground water, about *Mozart*, for heaven's sake—about anything that came to his mind. He collected coins, had begun a lifelong fascination with archaeology, built things just to see if they worked. He even built an electronic organ that he played with great pleasure for several years.

It may have been that year that Daddy decided that science could be used to make chicken-killing more humane. As I have said, we kept chickens for eggs, and sometimes Mother would kill them with a hatchet on the edge of our sandbox. (Mark and I would laugh for years about having to explain to friends why great gouts of blood were in our sandbox.) Daddy's idea was an electronic device that would pull a slender copper wire and garrotte a chicken with such speed that it could be painless. No dull whack from Mother's hatchet, just insert the chicken's head in a loop and flip a switch. I don't think the machine ever made it to clinical trials. Perhaps Daddy realized that if something went wrong, the device might cause more pain than we had a right to inflict anyway.

More memorable were the bombs Daddy made for his high school physics classes to demonstrate the speed of sound. Some people are born teachers, and the term might have been invented for my father, because he *never* stopped teaching. He went right from talking about the periodic table of the elements into a speech that might include detours around crystal formation and self-reliance. Something of a libertarian, he had no patience with anyone who wouldn't work hard for success. He would never have built bombs at all if they didn't offer instruction.

Daddy got empty pill boxes (in those days before plastic pill bottles), filled them with gunpowder, then taped them tightly with the white adhesive tape the football team used to wrap ankles and wrists. Then he'd insert a piece of thick orange dynamite fuse.

In these days of crazed bombers, it seems somewhat foolhardy, even suspicious, but in those more innocent times, nobody minded if the science teacher wanted to blow something up to demonstrate the speed of sound. (One rocket he built exploded too near his hand once, and he had to wear a bandage around it for weeks.)

But more than chemistry, more than chicken-killing machines, more than bombs, the science in our house was about electricity. In his book about the genius physicist Richard Feynman, science writer James Gleick said that most of the great scientists in the first half of the Twentieth Century first had a fascination either with chemistry or radio. My father apparently never decided between them. So if the newspaper ran a story about Christmas lights, my father would want to know how the blasted things were wired, not their color. He could have cared less what stations a short-wave radio picked up but was entranced by how the radio did it. He was constantly drawing diagrams and then building what to me were unimaginably complicated gizmos.

His greatest success (to me) was the construction of a Tesla coil, a cylinder wrapped with copper wire which, when turned on, sent a long spark from its top. (Think *Frankenstein*.) As usual with such projects, everything else went undone when he was working on it. The great coil slowly took painstaking shape, and when he finally tested it, the cylinder began to buzz with electricity, and a huge blue spark snapped from the top. I was scared at first, but he told me it was all right. I would have walked into the path of a chicken truck if he had said it was safe. Because it had a high voltage and low amperage, you could actually whisk your finger through the spark. I was scared to try it, though Mark, typically, wasn't. Finally, I did begin to make a few quick passes with my index finger, at first not even close to the spark, but then closer and closer until I actually did it. My father had no patience for things that did not work. To this day, I don't, either. He knew *how* they worked, so if they did not work, there had to be some malevolent force involved.

All of which is to explain Christmas tree lights.

In those days, the bulbs were in series. Anyone of a certain age knows what this means: if one burned out, they *all* went out. I suppose for some families it was a game—change bulbs until you find the one that turns the strand back on. (Unless *two* were burned out, a puzzle of utterly evil dimensions.) In my family, it was the cause for great waves of shouting. I always hated getting the Christmas tree lights out because I knew—as well as I knew anything—that they would not work. *Of course,* they wouldn't work. Daddy would untangle them while I silently prayed that they would blossom into beautiful reds and greens, but when he plugged them in—nothing. Year after year after year, when Christmas tree lights burned out, he knew it was personal, not accidental. More, it was a test. He would grumble, growl, start changing lights, saying it was hopeless, that he would have to spend money we didn't have, that the lights were probably made by morons.

And then, suddenly, gloriously, the strand would explode into light against the linoleum-covered floor. Joy would fill me. Once the lights were burning, there was no reason for more chemistry experiments, Tesla coils, or bombs.

Now, we could go into the woods to look for a Christmas tree.

fourteen

Every December, two or three weeks before Christmas, Daddy, Mark, and I would set out on a frosty Saturday morning and head for the woods. This was unusual because Daddy rarely came to the forest, being too busy with adult life. That year, Laura Jane was with us, and Mother exulted in the care of her new daughter, though Daddy doted, too. Since I was nine years older than the baby, whom we would come to call Lolly, I was not jealous of that attention. Besides, she was funny. She had huge blue eyes, laughed all the time, and loved to be held.

This trip was the most special of the year, when we went to hunt for the perfect Christmas tree. In the South there was only one true kind of Christmas tree: the cedar. The woods behind our house held a surprising number of fine cedars, from seedlings to huge ones with limbs reaching from sky to ground. Not only were cedars fine for climbing, they were ideal for hiding. The dense foliage, the close-packed limbs made them a perfect sanctuary. Often, when I was alone in the woods, I'd find a cedar to scale and stay up there for hours, listening to birds, pretending that Indian attack was imminent. It took a great deal of boredom for me to move much in those days. I could sit happily in one place for hours.

On one memorable trip for a Christmas tree, I think a year or two earlier, we had reached Rocky Island, where three creeks merged. At the edge of one small creek, Daddy told us to move back because he was going to try something. He paced off a distance from a large pine, balanced himself, raised the hatchet and threw it. It flew awkwardly, almost in slow motion, like a road sign tumbling in a storm. Then, with a resounding thwack, it struck, the blade digging into the punky bark. Mark and I stood amazed at the sight. Daddy's throwing arm was still extended toward the tree, and we were all frozen in shock and admiration for the beauty of that motion. (Years later, Mark and I would order some Wham-O! Malayan Throwing Knives from the back of an issue of *Boy's Life* and do considerable damage to trees in our back yard.)

This year was at least the fifth year in which we had gone scouting for a Christmas tree, and we were determined to find the best cedar in the forest.

The pine woods might have been my bones. I knew them by this time so well that I could have walked through them blindfolded without striking my head on a single trunk. There were hardwoods here and there, especially near Rocky Island, but mostly we played, camped, and lingered among the pines. I loved the pines, but I worshiped the cedars.

First was their aroma, one of the loveliest natural smells on earth. You could stand near one and simply inhale that delicious fragrance, almost sip it, feel it rich and pleasant on the tongue. I never passed a cedar tree without thrusting my face (carefully) into its branches and taking a good whiff. More often, I could find some small branch and break it off, bringing it slowly to my nose. I carried it with me for hours, bringing it up for a sniff from time to time.

Just as pleasing was their shape. Nothing else in the woods looked like a Christmas tree except the cedar, and that blue-green foliage held its shape against wind and rain. The limb structure was also perfect for a climbing boy.

Daddy walked slowly, keeping his eyes open. He would come up to a tree that might have a bad side or was too fat or thin.

"What do you think of this one, boys?" he might ask.

"I don't know," I'd say, disappointed that he was even considering it. *That* tree would look terrible in our front room near the piano.

"Well, with the lights on, it might look pretty good," he'd say, watching us from the corner of his eye.

"If the lights are still working," Mark might blurt.

"And some icicles," Daddy said. "We could cover up the bad spots with icicles."

Mark and I walked around the sad tree, feeling a bit downcast until Daddy, inevitably, smiled and told us to come on, that we could surely find a better tree than this in a whole forest. Mark and I whooped and dashed forward, on the lookout for the right cedar.

Finally, every year, Daddy somehow lead us to a spot deep in the woods, maybe farther than we normally ranged, and he would stop and point. And there, miraculously, unbelievably, was our Christmas tree. In my imagination and delight, I saw the right tree ringed in light, as if awaiting us in its sheer perfection. Then we walked around it, praising its shape, its aroma.

"What do you think of this one, boys?" Daddy then asked.

"*Unh huh!*" we'd cry.

Our breaths feathered the air. Daddy in his coat would kneel before the tree and lightly hack away the ground-hugging branches, then begin to cut it down. I watched with a rising joy, never once thinking of the tree we were killing but only of the beauty it would bring to our house. Once the Christmas tree was up and decorated, there was no doubt that the holiday was near.

So it was that December 1959. Mark and I watched as he finished chopping down the six-foot cedar and dragging it clear of the stump. He stood it on end and shook it three times to knock out loose and dead needles, and a small shower of cedar-leavings sifted beneath it. Then we turned and headed back through the woods toward the field and, across it, home.

Once the tree was in its stand, Daddy put on the lights. Finally, after an evening of fiddling with the tangled strands, they would work nicely. Daddy would strand them around the tree from top to bottom. I vaguely remember—did it happen at all?—Laura Jane sitting in her high chair and watching as we decorated the tree, and music from Handel's *Messiah* flowing gently in the background. We put on all the bulbs and balls that my parents had been collecting since their wedding in 1945. We boys broke so many that I suppose most weren't that old. We did have some plastic icicles with hooks on the end that had survived for years. The last of that pleasant chore (was Mother in the kitchen popping popcorn to eat afterward?) was the hanging of the stranded icicles.

Everyone is familiar with these shining strips, but in those days the icicles were made of lead instead of plastic. You could take two or three and crumple them up in your hand

and make a small silvery ball that, with repeated rubbings on a hard surface, would gleam. We had no idea that they were poisonous but I don't recall anyone eating any. Then, as the tree was finished and stood gleaming with promise in our front room, we celebrated with hot chocolate, and I felt a perfect joy. The details always seemed to be the same, but that year I was the least bit uncomfortable. We still had a state championship to win, and I had asked for a red football uniform.

The only problem, once the lovely cedar tree stood in our house, was the waiting.

fifteen

Snow fell in northeast Georgia on Sunday night, December 6. We were probably ninety miles away from it, but the sheer mention of Christmas and snow in the same sentence sent us all into a speculative frenzy. *The Atlanta Constitution* in its Monday morning edition said it would be "as cold as the frost on a mint julep glass."

The day before, the New York Giants had pounded the Cleveland Browns for their second straight Eastern conference title. Charley Connerly threw for three touchdowns. The Browns' best player, running back Jim Brown, was hurt early in the game and missed most of it. The paper reported that King Valentine, the horse of old cowboy star William S. Hart, had died in California. Violin virtuoso David Oistrakh was playing in Atlanta. Life moved on.

If we had Ray Bennett, the "dazzling 138-pound flash" in our backfield, Brooks County had a halfback named Howard Daughtry, who weighed 185. Even at nine, I could add. We were going to get killed, humiliated. Since Daddy was principal of the school, he would be shamed, too. I cannot account, forty years later, for thinking such a thing, but I did. I began to realize that winning this championship was personal to me, that I would barely be able to face my schoolmates if we lost. Somehow, it became my responsibility to *make* the Bulldogs win. That week of the game, the town was in a complete uproar. There were pep rallies and ribbon sales. The banks paid for chartered buses—a fine service and smart business.

The weather warmed up all that week, and by Friday morning rain was falling, and a high in the low 60s was expected. I was beside myself with anxiety for the team, somewhat resigned. Any team with a 185-pound halfback would probably be impossible to beat. (I tried to imagine 185 pounds, and I could see a giant with tree trunks for legs.)

Brooks County lies flat against the state line between Georgia and Florida. The game was at Fort Valley High School, a neutral field about eighty miles south of Madison and one hundred and twenty-five miles north of Quitman, the county seat of Brooks County. Rain began to fall and fog crept up one end of the stadium. I huddled miserably in the rain, thinking of my football uniform, wondering vaguely if I wouldn't get it should we lose. That made sense. Instead, I might get clothes or the ultimate punishment for bad boys in those days, switches and coal. I was always afraid I'd look in my stocking and find sooty lumps of coal, final proof of my badness.

The field was soaked, and it was soon clear that neither team could hold on to the ball. We forced an early drive, with Neal Vason doing most of the damage from fullback, but then we fumbled. Brooks County drove down to our six-yard line just before half when they fumbled and Charles Bell recovered it. At halftime, we were staring with disbelief at a scoreless tie. The Bulldogs had scored more than forty points five times that season.

The rain came down straight in strands. No one scored in the third quarter, either, and the tension and screaming in the stands was deafening. Late in the fourth quarter with a scoreless tie still on the boards, we began a brilliant drive that left us, finally, with fourth down and three on the Brooks County five-yard-line. This was the game and everybody in the stands knew it.

We ran off tackle, and the referee signaled for a measurement. I could hardly see what was happening but I knew the game would turn on whether or not we made the first down. Suddenly I saw the Brooks County fans across the field begin to go wild, arms up in unison, and I felt my legs buckle. I sat down. We had missed the first down by inches. I could see the title slipping away. Still, we had a fabulous defense, and perhaps we could force a punt for field position before time ran out. Brooks County lined up. I held my breath.

Then, as unexpected as southern snow, a miracle occurred. Brooks County's back fumbled the ball, and it bounced into the arms of our Bonar Newton on the six-yard-line, and he took three steps and found himself standing in the end zone. Our stands exploded—literally, it seemed to me. I screamed myself hoarse. Neal Vason ran in the extra point, and we led 7-0. On its next possession, Brooks County couldn't move against our defense, and the game ended on a long Morgan County drive.

We had done it, won the state title for the fourth time in five years. My elation knew no bounds, and I tried to see celebration on the field, but everyone was jumping up and down in front of me. Between the hugging and backslapping, when my sight-lines were clear, I saw a mass of red football uniforms in the rain, leaping higher and higher on each other, as if in victory they might well reach the lower stars.

sixteen

Christmas weather where we lived in north central Georgia was unpredictable. Some years, the sky cleared and a deep, heavy cold settled in, though rarely with any snow. A white Christmas was something you saw on a Currier & Ives card or television.

My parents by then had been married fourteen years. The story of their courtship is a classic, a wartime romance in which the man and woman were thousands of miles apart. My father, before the war, had been friends with Harmon Sisk in Seneca, and Daddy knew that Harmon had a kid sister named Ruth, but they did not really begin to notice each other until my father was home from the war on a medical furlough for a week. They spent considerable time together that week and then began a long courtship by letter.

My father was stationed at Mount Farm, an Army Air Force Base near Oxford in the English countryside. Mother joined the Navy as a WAVE and spent much of the early war as a postal clerk in New York City. My father was mustered out three months after VJ day in 1945. The Navy had transferred Mother to San Francisco and she was still in service, so when Daddy came home to Seneca, he then took a bus across America, and he and my mother were married in the First Baptist Church of San Francisco on November 17, 1945.

That first Christmas after their marriage, they lived with my mother's parents in Seneca, and when they awoke, snow was falling, and the ground was a lovely white. Perhaps it was an omen for a good life and a long marriage. In November 1998 they would celebrate their 53rd wedding anniversary.

Two weeks before Christmas 1959, the low hovered near freezing, but in the afternoons, the temperature rose into the mid-fifties on Monday and then near sixty on Tuesday. Not Christmas weather. This was in the days before long-range forecasts, so no one had a clue what would happen by Christmas Day. I wanted a white Christmas, wanted to see snowflakes falling slowly from that southern sky. Snow was rare enough in Georgia so that when snow began people would rush to their windows to watch. But that year we mostly had rain and fog and no hint of ice. We usually had most of our ice in February and March, anyway, so I guessed a white Christmas was completely out of the question.

That week after the state championship game, I played with my old worn out football. I would often play sandlot football with friends, and perhaps we played some that week, though I cannot remember it. Already, unimaginably, the town was moving on to other things. Madison's Christmas lights were up and shining. Contractors put the finishing touches on our new hospital, which would open for patients on January 1, 1960. *The Madisonian* printed the first two-color edition in its history.

We had a dilemma about the Christmas parade. My father obviously would be going to the band concert, and I wanted to go, too, so we compromised. We'd visit the parade for a while and then dash back to the high school for seasonal music.

That night of December 17 was cool and foggy. Santa's throne on the porch of the Courthouse was roped to keep surging kids back, and Boy Scouts dressed as elves handed out fruit and candy. I remember being startled by this parade with no band—just Christmas music blaring over a loud-speaker.

Across the town square at the Madison Theatre, a Friday night double feature was planned: *That Kind of Woman* with Sophia Loren and Tab Hunter and *I Was a Teenage Werewolf* with the very young Michael Landon. The Saturday double feature was even less seasonal: *Valerie* with blond bombshell Anita Ekberg and *A King and Four Queens* with Clark Gable and Eleanor Parker. We hung out at the parade for a while, though I wouldn't go near Santa Claus—at nine I was too old for such foolishness. Then we headed back to the high school for the band concert.

All the concerts I saw in the auditorium have melted together in my mind over the decades, like records left in the sun. That year's event is lost to memory, but I know that I was allowed to wander among the instrument cases back stage and inhale their pleasant fragrance, to watch as Mr. Redwine gave the downbeat and started our award-winning band. I was surprised to feel myself sliding away from the world of football. There was nothing more for the school to prove that year, so the band would have to excel next. I had been to many plays and concerts in that auditorium.

It was that autumn, I think, that we had seen a magician perform there. I was sitting in the audience with Daddy when the fellow came off stage, out among us, and began to go through a pickpocket routine. My father had a large fountain pen—the kind with a lever to siphon ink from a bottle. He dearly loved it, used it to sign dozens of forms and letters, the duty of a high school principal. When the magician came to us, he engaged in a bit of hammy misdirection and snatched the fountain pen from inside my father's coat.

"Hey!" I cried, pointing to the pen, but Daddy grabbed my arm and smiled.

"I'll get it back," he whispered. I watched, astonished, as the pickpocket went through a few more people, just as clumsily taking things from them. Then he dashed on stage and with a vaudevillian flourish began to reveal the items one by one, inviting the owners to come up and get them. Daddy sent me forward to retrieve his pen, but the whole thing smelled of a hoax to me. I don't think the magician fooled anybody.

The last event of the evening involved the magician catching between his teeth a .22 bullet fired from a rifle by his assistant. The act was dramatic, his rousing finale, and utterly unbelievable. People applauded, but no one was impressed. Perhaps it was just a chance to suspend our disbelief, like going to the movies. The evening of the concert, however, was far more special, for the art and craft of band music were quite real.

Some day, I thought, I'd like to sit up there. I'd like to make that kind of sound for the holidays.

seventeen

Classical music has always been like breath to my father. I doubt there has been a day in the past sixty-five years that he has not listened to it. Though long-playing records had been available since the late 1940s, we had only a few until much later. We did, however, have a handsome collection of 78s in their *albums*—a term that meant something with those heavy shellac discs. Even a symphony of standard length might take seven or eight discs.

But the Queen Mother of our collection was Handel's *Messiah*. In all, there were thirty-eight sides in the set. To play them, my father had built our own record player, a huge beast with a large speaker. Most players in those days were cramped and tinny, yappy as a small dog. Our record player could fill a large room with sound. Every Christmas we listened to the discs as my father sat nearby, changing records as they sped to a finish.

It was in that Christmas season, just after we had won the state championship, that my father decided we would lug the massive record player from our house to the high school auditorium. He wanted to set it up and play, for anyone who wished to come, Handel's *Messiah*—a gift to the community that still operated on the broad back of the land, a place where farmers were our most important citizens. The weekend passed, and I was excited about the event, because it was a classy gesture, an offering of culture.

On Tuesday evening, December 22, I went with Daddy to the high school, watching him lug the two-volume set of the *Messiah*. In those days he was painfully thin but strong, and the muscles in his arms went taut against the weight. Even at nine, I knew this was a fine and decent act, expressing both his altruism and his deep love for music. I imagined that dozens, maybe hundreds, would start filtering in, that at the end they would thank him—thank *me*—for this marvelous Christmas gift.

I knew the auditorium well, its dark purple curtains with gold fringes and square stage, its fold-up wooden seats bearing everything from intertwined lovers' initials to dates. In fact, I knew the high school best from the period *after* school, when Mark and I had the run of all the buildings. The silence of an empty building addicted me, just like the open world of a quiet field, the sacristy of a stream in a silent forest. The janitors, like Dairy Henderson, were good friends. I grew to love motionless things and that deep stillness. In 1956, I had been the mascot of the Thespian Society and had to make a little speech just before the curtains parted on a production of *Meet Me in St. Louis*. My entire speech: "Hello folks, we're glad you're here, to see us dance and sing. I'm the mascot of the year. Thank you folks for everything." The drama teacher, Alma Quillian, wrote it for me. She also taught math, and years later gently led me into and out of algebra and trig, passing me, even though I was a miserable student. For being the mascot, I got a huge box of Lincoln Logs which I treasured for years.

My father and Mark had brought the record player to the auditorium earlier, and so Daddy placed the record albums on a chair next to it and went off to turn on the heat. The place was freezing, but my father wasn't the kind to waste the county's money heating it during an afternoon when nobody was there. Everybody could just be cool until it warmed up. I went to the broad stand of windows to watch for cars. He had told the newspaper about the concert, but they hadn't run anything. (Mark stayed home with Mother and Lolly.)

Rain began to fall. Streaks of cold water spread down the windows, branched like leafless trees. I kept my coat on, even my black cap with cottony ear muffs, as I waited for the crowd. We were forty minutes early, so there was plenty of time. Suddenly, the building seemed to shudder and give a great sigh as the heat came on. I smiled and slipped from my coat and draped it over a seat near the back. The place would be packed, and I didn't want to seem presumptuous by sitting down front. Maybe it would seem like bragging. I had been taught from my earliest memory that good deeds are diminished if you take pride in them. My father and mother would spend their lives doing things for others but they never, ever, displayed any pride for it. Even today when someone praises me for anything, I tend to cringe.

I went back to the windows to watch for headlights. My father came in and out of the auditorium, puttering around. He was a world-class putterer, never able to sit still, always off looking for something else to explore, and that trait would blossom in Mark but would miss me. My father can repair anything and so can Mark. If it takes more than duct tape, I'm at sea. Ten minutes passed, then half an hour. A few minutes before show time, nobody had come.

I began to suffer as I watched my father wait for people to

hear the glorious choruses and solos of Handel. Of course he loved the standard "big" pieces like the chorus "Hallelujah," but his favorites were such arias as "I Know That My Redeemer Liveth." I ran back to the windows and began to beg for someone to come—*anybody*. Madison was not an uncultured town by any means. Suddenly I saw a smear of headlights across the dripping window panes.

"I think somebody's coming!" I cried.

"Don't get excited," said my father. "Let's just see." The car swung past the auditorium, slowed, then disappeared into the night. The only sound was rain and my father's footsteps on the hollow stage. I felt an emptiness fill me, a terrible and expanding embarrassment. *Where were they? Why had they not come?* The minutes thudded past, and we waited for some time. My father didn't seem to mind, since he found plenty to keep him occupied. All I could do was wait. Fifteen minutes past the announced time, nobody had come. Thirty minutes after it, nobody had come.

Finally, my father disappeared into the back, and a few moments later the heat stopped breathing, like an old man giving up and dying without a struggle. I walked to the back of the auditorium and got my coat and ear-muff hat, came down front just as my father was turning out lights and picking up the precious record albums.

"Why didn't anybody come?" I asked. He didn't seem especially worried but I was sick with shame.

"It's a bad night, and they probably had other things to do," he said. "I'll get the record player tomorrow, and we can listen to it at home."

"Yes, sir," I said miserably. He turned the last lights out and locked the doors, and we hurried to the car through the rain. I pulled my coat to me in the darkness and he drove us home, humming. I looked out into the night during our thirty-second drive back past the Teacherage to our house. I had imagined a report of magnificent success, but it was not to be.

Two days later, *The Madisonian*, unbelievably, ran this story on the front page:

A special treat is in store for music lovers of Morgan County Tuesday evening, December 22. Marshall Williams will present a music program of Handel's Messiah at the high school auditorium. Mr. Williams said the public was invited to the performance which will be free. The music will be presented on high fidelity. Mr. Williams said the arrangement as recorded is beautiful and that he wishes to share the music with the public.

I was impressed that the story had made the front page, but this was the issue of Thursday, December 24—*two days late*. I was too young to understand the pressures under which weekly newspaper editors work and that such errors sometimes just happened. (Fifteen years later, I would return to Madison to work for that paper and its publisher and editor, Graham and Adelaide Ponder. They became my mentors and friends.) As I recall, Daddy didn't say anything about it. In the end, he got to listen to the *Messiah* again by himself at home, and that was enough joy at Christmas.

eighteen

As Christmas eve came upon us, the weather took a sharp turn colder. The highs were in the forties, and since school was out, Mark and I played all day as I worried about getting my football uniform. Football season just wouldn't quite end. Neal Vason, Bonar Newton, and Jerry Hillsman were named to the All-State team, and five others were listed as honorable mention. I thought: *Just wait until the 1960 season. We're going to win again, and I'll be on the sideline with a year's practice in my red football uniform.*

In addition to running the story about the *Messiah* that week, the paper announced the following in the "personals" section:

> *The Marshall Williams will spend the Christmas holiday in Seneca, S. C., with Mrs. Williams parents, Mr. and Mrs. Lee Sisk.*

This now seems utterly bizarre—that we would announce to everyone in Morgan County that we would not be at home for a number of days around Christmas—a blank invitation to burglars. In truth, we probably could have left the doors wide open and nothing would have gone missing. The social innocence of those days was a dying thing, but none of us knew it then.

That day before Christmas, Mother packed as usual for our few days in Seneca. Christmas was always bittersweet in a way—I wanted to stay home and exult in my bounty and play at my own house. Then again, we got presents in Seneca, too, and I got to see my relatives, whom I loved. And so we boys would have time to play with our toys for maybe an hour, then we'd eat, dress, and hit the road.

I recall those drives so well, because there were very few cars on the road. Daddy would tune the radio to a religious service, the news, some music. We had a book of quiz questions we bought along, and if we could get Daddy to turn off the radio, we'd ask them aloud. Also, we'd beg Daddy to ask us questions about chemistry, electronics, music—almost anything. We were always interested in facts.

There was another reason for celebration, though. This was my sister Laura Jane's first Christmas. In the Bible my parents had given me several years earlier, my name embossed in gold on the black cover, there was a picture of the baby Jesus lying in the manger, wise men attending. The usual iconographic light played over the scene. I would sit and stare at that picture for long minutes, thinking of the Christ child and his penury.

Looking back from the vantage of these many years, I can see that we shared a lack of money as well. The floor of our house was bitterly cold in winter, so Daddy bought a large rug to cover part of it. When the winter winds blew, though, the rug then lifted off the floor beneath us, rising from cold air. Thus the rug waffled, sometimes trapping the cold air, sometimes letting it out. In those days, I had no ideas of privation, though. We had a large garden each summer, and we owned books and music and a thousand interesting things.

This Christmas was different, though, because we had a baby, too, just like the family of Mary and Joseph. I looked upon Laura Jane with wonder. Mother would let me sit on the couch and hold her sometimes, but I was afraid I'd break her and begged off.

As I said, the shotgun hallway had originally gone straight through the house, but a couple of years before, it had been partitioned. Daddy moved the bunk beds Mark and I used from the front room to the area behind the partition which was easier and cheaper to heat. Laura Jane slept in her crib in my parents' bedroom which adjoined. And so that Christmas, there were five of us crammed into two cold rooms, and another stocking was placed on the mantel for my sister.

Mother usually let us open one gift on Christmas eve to keep us calm. Some years, even that didn't work. She recalls one time—probably earlier than 1959—when by midnight Mark and I still could not fall asleep in our excitement. So she made and brought us hot chocolate, talked to us in her quiet, soothing voice, and soon we were both asleep. This Christmas was special, though. The Morgan County Bulldogs had won the state championship, and in only a few years, I would be there to help them. And so I went to sleep, hoping that somehow something as elaborate as a red football uniform might find its way into our house.

Mark and I awoke early, but we knew better than to roam out through the den and into the front room where the tree and our presents lay. So we waited, making coughing noises, whispering and talking, until Mother and Daddy got up, bringing the drowsy baby with them.

71

✳

"Can we please go see if Santa Claus came?" I begged, knowing the truth about that hallowed old man but unwilling to say it aloud for fear his bounty might vanish.

"Let me turn on the lights," Daddy said. He disappeared into the front room, and, standing in the doorway, I could see the glow from the Christmas tree lights. I felt myself trembling, wanted to rush in, wanted to go back to bed. Then: "Y'all can come on in."

Mark went first, being the oldest (and strongest), and I did not see what he got. My eyes widened in shock: Beneath the tree, in spread-out splendor was the most marvelous football uniform I could have imagined, with all the pads separate, even knee pads and hip pads. But there was more. Next to them was a new football and a kicking tee.

"Look! Look!" I cried.

I felt upon my uniform hungrily, touching each piece, especially the red helmet. I lifted it in that cold light and placed it upon my head as Charlemagne must have been crowned. I did not see what my brother got, what toys my sister received. I couldn't turn to the stockings. I began, in a wild rush, to put the uniform on over my pajamas. Daddy helped me with the shoulder pads, lacing them up. Finally, blessedly, I was dressed and had my football under my arm, and the new tee in my hand. I was going outside. Nothing could have stopped me. I thought about putting on the old cleated football shoes I had, but I knew I couldn't kick well in them, so I walked toward the door barefooted.

"Get some shoes on," Mother said.

"I can't kick in shoes," I cried. *"Please?"*

She must have seen the naked longing in my eyes, and Laura Jane was in her arms anyway, so she just nodded, and I went into the hall, opened the front door and stepped into heaven.

The grass was bent and spiky with the cold. I inhaled, felt the cold air rush into my lungs, walked to the side yard and placed my tee on the ground. The football did not have a bladder like my discarded one from the high school. This one was rubber, inflated tight to bursting, perhaps somewhat too fat, but I loved it. The sun was coming up from behind the house, casting long shadows from the pecan trees and from the fence posts that separated our house from the pastures. I leaned down and placed the football on the tee, stood back up and backed off two steps.

There are three seconds left in the game, and the Bulldogs have called a time out. Coach Corry is talking to the team and it looks like . . . yes, he's sending Phil Williams in to kick. With the state title on the line, he's showing a lot of confidence in that young man. Williams has had a good year, but can he make a field goal this long and win it all? He seems confident, though. Now they're lining up, and Williams touches the holder on the helmet and nods, steps back. Here's the snap . . . and the kick . . . and it's . . . good! Phil Williams has just won the state championship!

And I kicked and my bare foot sank into the rubber ball, and it exploded from my foot, rising and rising, end over end, going ten, twenty, thirty yards, entirely over the privet hedge and deep into the back yard. I raised my arms high over my head, and in my nine-year-old imagination heard the shouts of thousands.

There are few moments in life we can call *perfect*, the ideal blending of hope and desire, that place where dreams turn suddenly and wonderfully into truth, but that morning was born in perfection. I retrieved the ball, kicked over and over again, each time higher and farther, until I thought I could bounce it off Orion's belt.

I wore my football uniform on the two-hour drive to Seneca that morning, running through Bulldog football games in my mind. What position would I play when the time came? Fullback, probably, because I was a bit lumbering though I could take a hit. I could tell how it all began back in 1959 when I got my first red football uniform, and it brought me into the real world of sports, when I grew confidence.

When we finally got there, Papa took one look at me and grinned.

"Good granny's alive, boy, what you got on?" he said, slapping me on the back.

"It's got all the pads just like the bigger ones," I said.

Then, ignoring everyone else, I went into my grandmother's back yard and played a team sport by myself until, hours later, hunger drove me indoors. I repeated the same peacock display at Aunt Ben's house, running in her long back yard and kicking the ball as she stood in the yard and smiled with her typical complete joy in small things.

This was the perfect Christmas, the perfect year. My life was awash with sheer delight.

It was very cold that winter, and at the end of January, I turned ten and felt I was nearly grown. I could imagine high school graduation, with Daddy presenting me my diploma, and I could see no reason why that would not happen for me and the class of 1968. But ten-year-olds know nothing of that grown-up world which surrounds and envelops them, cannot anticipate or fend off the world coming at them. Football season faded away, and 1960 seemed calm and bright at our house on Old Buckhead Road. I continued to play in the yard, but I also dressed early on cold Saturday mornings and walked to the high school where I kicked and ran on the football field in a misty silence. Somehow, against sense, I was coming to associate football and my beloved uniform with the quiet, still morning. I narrated my own exploits out loud. The phantoms in the empty stands cheered me. The world had turned to basketball, but I wouldn't let go of football, could not.

In early March, when the jonquils were blossoming and spring whispered in the fields, Daddy sat us down one evening for a serious talk. He took his fatherly duties as a trust between us, and I knew from his voice something urgent was imminent. Mark and I sat on the sofa in the den. Mother and Lolly were in the kitchen.

"Boys, I need to tell you something important," he said slowly. "I'm going to be leaving my job at the high school at the end of this school year." He continued to talk, but I heard nothing, stunned and confused. Leave the high school? That was not possible. We practically *owned* the high school. We did anything we pleased — slid down the old-fashioned tube fire escapes, walked into the band room during practice.

"What are you going to do?" Mark asked.

"I'm looking at several different things right now," he said. "Of course, you know the board of education owns this house. It's for the high school principal and his family, so we'll have to move."

"We won't still live here?" I asked, frightened even to think of the answer.

"No, son," Daddy repeated. "We'll have to move. I'm not sure yet where we'll be going. There's a chance it could be South Carolina. That would be okay, wouldn't it?"

"I guess so."

"At any rate, we can live here for a while yet until they hire a new principal. We're not going anywhere soon."

"Yes, sir."

That was all we needed to know for the time being, but I felt a clammy fear, a realization that my woods and pastures, that everything I knew and loved would suddenly disappear. We would become vagabonds. I would never again head to the woods to cut a Christmas cedar with my father and brother.

That week, my father's picture was on the front page of *The Madisonian* with his picture, saying he had resigned as principal at Morgan County High School. While he had not publically divulged the reasons for leaving, the paper read between the lines with ease in its editorial:

> *The people of Morgan County learned with regret this week of the resignation of Marshall Williams from the faculty of Morgan County High School. Mr. Williams is certainly one of Morgan County's better teachers . . . he will leave his position to seek another job in what he calls "the best interest of my family."*
>
> *Mr. Williams is one of hundreds, even thousands, who are leaving their teaching jobs this year. A sad commentary on the great exodus from the classrooms of Georgia is the fact that these teachers are leaving often among the state's best qualified and finest . . .*
>
> *Too often their reasons are similar: although they are educated to teach and they love their profession, they can make a much better living elsewhere . . . we deeply regret the loss of Mr. Williams [and] we think his loss indicative of the times.*

I half believed the crisis would pass, but when I saw his picture in the paper, I knew it was true. We would have to leave our home. I imagined us wayward wanderers, living in different towns, I wondered if fields or woods might be near. I sadly folded my football uniform and put it up, because I assumed I would never play now for the great Morgan County Bulldogs.

An ice storm swept into the county that same week, the worst since the late 1930s, and power lines bent down like old humped men beneath the frozen weight. The electricity went off, and friends from the Teacherage came to our house because we had a working fireplace, and they didn't. We huddled in the front room against the bitter cold and waited for it to melt. When the wind blew, even the bushes crackled beneath their coated weight. That same week, the boiler of a laundry downtown exploded and blew out most of the storefront windows in Madison. No one was hurt, but it took two days to sweep up all the glass. One huge hunk of iron from the boiler was found more than five hundred yards away, but by the miracle of chance, no one got hurt.

Then on Thursday, March 10, a thick, heavy snow began to fall at dusk. We assumed it would fade by midnight, and so were stunned to awaken that next morning to find school had been canceled and eight inches of snow had filed the edges from our southern landscape. Snow fell perhaps twice a year in Madison, but I had never seen this much. We instantly forgot the worries of moving and went into the yard that morning to play.

The storm swept our world clean. Blooming jonquils in our yard sank in silence. The red-rutted ditches of our pasture were a silky white. I could see my words in that air. Our dog, Flipsy, loved the snow, kicking around like a lamb in spring grass, and she followed us wherever we went. Mother had set out my coat and gloves, along with the ear-flap hat I'd worn the night of the *Messiah*. My world lifted with pleasure in the glory of snow.

The local radio station, WYTH, decided to have a snowman contest, and we boys and our friends decided to win it. Our friend David Belcher, who lived farther out Old Buckhead Road, and the brothers Roy and Jack Lindsey joined Mark and me in the Lindsey front yard, and we went to work.

I do not recall who came up with the idea, but it was a good one: twin snow people we'd christen George and Martha Washington. (That was perhaps the only ice monument of the first First Lady ever made, certainly in Georgia.) We would appeal to the judges' patriotism and their sense of whimsy. We joined the snow people hand to hand using a cut off broomstick as a guide, and soon we had finished, positive that we would win. We should have known better.

Some of the older boys in town made a snowman that appealed to something far deeper in the southern psyche than George and Martha Washington. They built *Snowball* Jackson, holding an actual gun and standing in for famed Confederate General Stonewall Jackson. We were doomed, and we knew it. Still, George and Martha won second place in the contest, and for it we got passes to the Madison Theatre (at a time when a kids' ticket was, I think, twenty-five cents.) No matter. We were winners, and we went happily.

Soon enough, the sun came out and melted that lovely scene, though the snowmen all over town lingered for several days, even in the warmth of early spring. Finally, they, too disappeared, and we went back to school.

I tried to make sense of what had happened, and in some moments I even felt adventurous and excited. I always felt somewhat separated from my friends because none of our relatives were around, and now I felt even more distant. I only knew that football season was over and that I would never spend another Christmas in the only home I had ever known.

twenty

In late March, the school board announced they had hired Thomas Riden from Buford (though a native of Morgan County) to succeed Daddy as principal of Morgan County High School. The Riden family would be moving to Madison in late summer, and so we had until then to stay in our house.

The school year finally ended, and Mark and I launched ourselves on another summer, with Little League, cookouts, and camping trips to our woods. We had not begun packing, and Daddy didn't tell us much more about where we would move. I could see myself moving to Seneca to be with Mama and Papa and Aunt Ben and Uncle Chris—with cousins and family I had scarcely known.

What I did not suspect was that we would move to a house in town, there in Madison. When, in mid-July, we were told what was happening, I was overwhelmed with happiness and yet sad, for we would be leaving our life in the country. The "move to town" has become almost a southern myth— that escape from rural life to the new world of commerce. Our culture almost always thought it a step toward success.

My father's parents were the first generation of the Williams family to leave the farm, and Grandfather Williams (though I never knew him) ran a café and later a shoe repair shop in Seneca before his early death in 1935. But for me, bred to the fields and to solitude, that move was difficult, and it would take me months, if not years, to adjust.

We began to pack. The school year was not far away, and the Riden family needed the house. We found a small house on Poplar Street in Madison where the family of Phil Neugebauer had just moved out. Phil was a pharmacist, artist, writer, and raconteur—a man of extraordinary talents. But the house was cramped, and I was used to the huge drafty rooms of the "old house" as we would soon begin to call it. If I was worried, I was not afraid, because we had a family. Daddy said everything was fine, and it never occurred to me to doubt it. Mother, the rock of our lives, kept us charged up with her delicious sense of humor and organizational skills. Laura Jane, oblivious to the move, was a complete delight as always.

On August 1—Mark's twelfth birthday—we moved from our home on the country's edge to the house in town, and I left behind the only world I had ever known. I would not be able to play football for my Daddy at high school. He was no longer there. I had no claim to playing in the empty buildings or hanging out on Saturday mornings at the silent stadium.

And so we left behind our house and yard forever, and took with us our memories of Christmases spent in the country. This was printed in *The Madisonian* that week, one small paragraph among the personals:

Mr. and Mrs. Thomas Riden and daughters have arrived from Buford and will make their home here in the house near the high

*school campus formerly occupied by the Marshall Williams. The
Williams have moved into the house vacated by the Phil Neugebauers
on Poplar Street.*

And so that last country Christmas passed outside our
knowing. That world was slipping from us even though we'd
only moved two miles. Still, we had the world of Mama and
Papa and Aunt Ben in Seneca, we had Madison and friends,
and we had each other. We would survive. We lived on Poplar
Street only a couple of years before moving to a fine white
house around the corner on Foster Street.

A week or two after we moved, I rode my bicycle late one
afternoon back to the "old house" to check on the fields and
woods. I pumped past the house and entered a small dirt road
in the pasture just beyond where Mark and I had played
baseball all those long summers. I got off my bike and sat in
the pasture and inhaled the rich aroma of grass and cows and
soil and the nearby pine forest. For the first time since that
spring, I felt some contentment. This place would not
change, not for a long time. I could come here any time I
wanted to, even though I knew I would always be a visitor.

I thought for a long time of the journeys into the woods
for that perfect cedar tree for Christmas, how its fragrance, its
delicate structure, cheered the entire house at Christmas. My
red football uniform no longer seemed quite so important,
and it would be put away or given away or simply lost to time.

And so as I sat there and watched the first stars come out,
moved to tears by loss and affection, I felt as if I might rise
into those galaxies from the sheer joy of seeing that land
again. I began to hum the old Christmas hymn that I had
sung in church a hundred times but which I'd never connected
to my own world:

O Little town of Bethlehem, how still we see thee lie;
Above thy deep and dreamless sleep, the silent stars go by.

The world was not about winning football titles or living on a certain piece of land. It was about family, about a still, small town and its countryside, about the enduring and silent stars above it. Even though I had spent my last Christmas in the country, it would always be there in memory for me to visit. I sensed, perhaps for the first time, that my life was not about where I lived but about who I was.

Full of peace, I smiled and stretched, hands holding up the constellations, and then I rode my bicycle through the gathering night back toward town, toward home.

The starry, silent field behind Philip Lee Williams'
childhood home in Madison, Georgia.

*In 1991, Philip Lee Williams, his wife, and son moved to a house
on a dirt road in Oconee County, Georgia, not twenty miles from
where he grew up. Seven months after arriving, they rejoiced over
the birth of a daughter. Phil's brother Mark and his family live
only a mile away on another dirt road. Both their houses are sur-
rounded by a deep forest.*